To:

From:

Copyright 2019. All Rights Reserved. No part of this publication may be reproduced, or stored in a retrieval system, or transmitted by any form or by any means, electronic, mechanical, photocopying, recording or otherwise, without written permission, except in the context of reviews.

To my biggest supporters of
whatever I do in life,
a.k.a
The Knebel Team!

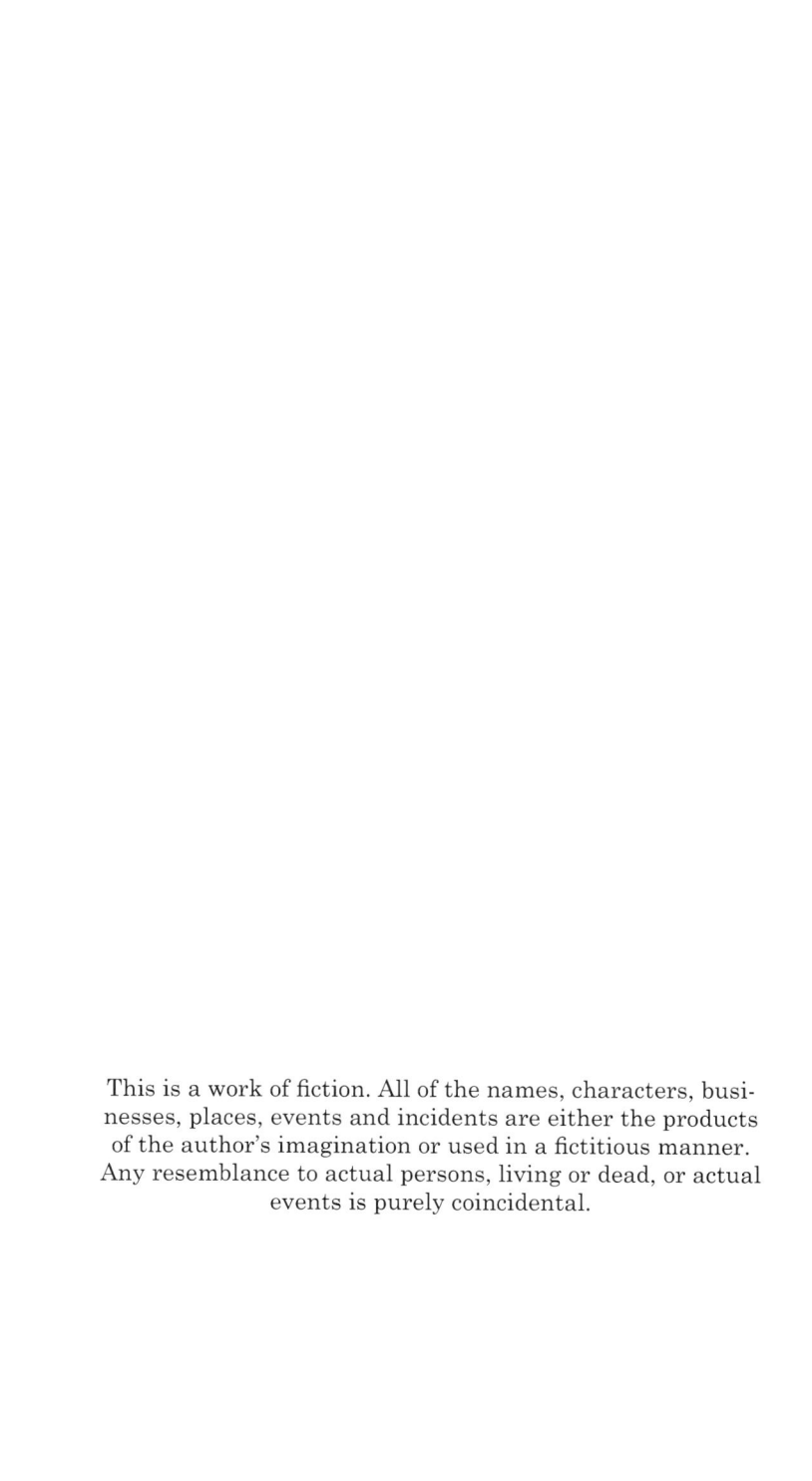

This is a work of fiction. All of the names, characters, businesses, places, events and incidents are either the products of the author's imagination or used in a fictitious manner. Any resemblance to actual persons, living or dead, or actual events is purely coincidental.

SPELLING PEN BRASS LAMP Book #3

by C. Knebel
Simple Words Books™

FREE DECODABLE
PHONICS WORKBOOK
and
FREE ACCESS TO ONLINE SUMMITS

simplewordsbooks.com

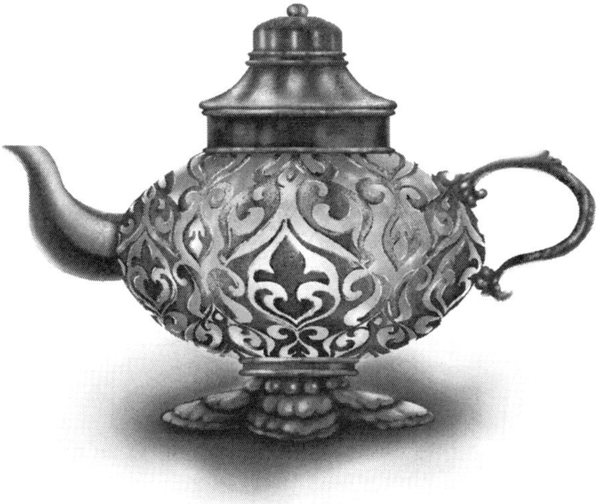

Chapter 1
Back To Elf Land

Matt stands in front of a mass of sand in Obelisk Land just where the Red Obelisk was.

"Elf King Gris and his tricks!" Liz says.

"That skunk must be planning his next plot. We must stop him just as we did with Basilisk Krig," Matt insists. "I bet King Gris will not stop his plans."

"Next, we must go back to Elf Land," Grandma Deb tells the kids. "We must check on the elf clan. When we were last in Elf Land with Basilisk Krig, not an elf was left at the huts."

Matt brings out the Spelling Pen to cast a spell.

He jots: 'Bring us back to Elf Land.'

The pen glints in Matt's hands.

A mist fills Obelisk Land. Matt, Liz and Grandma Deb link hands and vanish into the fog.

Matt is ten and his sibling Liz is six. They are the Sun Kids that stand up for Elf Land.

The Spelling Pen casts spells when Matt jots his wish. It was a gift to Matt from Grandma Deb.

The pen led Matt and Liz on big quests. When Elf Land was at risk, the Sun Kids got help from a bunch of goblins, imps and the elf clan to stop the bad king.

This quest got Matt to grasp the fact that all he had to do was his best.

With a big flash, Matt's spell brings them to Elf Land. They stand in the big thicket next to the path to the elf clan.

In a bit, an elf steps out of the thicket.

"Liz? Matt? Is that you?" he asks.

"Twigs!" yell Matt and Liz.

They run up to him.

"How are you?" asks Matt. "Where is the rest of the elf clan? Where is Mell?"

"We are all well. I have so much to tell you. Basilisk Krig was in Elf Land. We hid from him in the thicket," Twigs says.

He stops when he spots Grandma Deb. "And this is…"

"This is Grandma Deb," Matt says. "The Spelling Pen was a gift from her. She was a Sun Kid just as we are."

Twigs nods at Grandma Deb. "Glad to have you in Elf Land."

"She was on a quest in Elf Land as well when she was a kid," Liz jumps in. "Tell Twigs what you did in Elf Land, Grandma Deb."

"Back then, Basilisk Krig ran Elf Land," she tells him. "All were at risk. I went to Elf Land to help the griffins."

"The griffins!" Twigs gasps.

"Yes! We hid the Red Obelisk in Obelisk Land," she adds. "Then Basilisk Krig left Elf Land and things went well until King Gris. That is when Matt got the Spelling Pen as a gift."

Chapter 2
The Quest in Obelisk Land

"Basilisk Krig was in Elf Land!" Twigs grunts. "But then he just left. Was that you that got him out of Elf Land?" he asks.

"It was us!" Liz brags.

"King Gris and Basilisk Krig were in Obelisk Land," Matt says.

"Obelisk Land!" Twigs gasps.

Matt nods. "They dug out the Red Obelisk."

"Did you get rid of Basilisk Krig?" Twigs shrills.

"Well, in fact, it was King Gris that got rid of him," Matt shrugs.

"King Gris did that?" This stuns

Twigs. "Do not tell me he got a wish from the Red Obelisk."

"No, he did not," Liz says. "And Grandma Deb hid the Red Obelisk in the end. It sank back into the sand."

"I cannot think what King Gris will do if he gets a wish from the obelisk," Matt squints.

"King Gris did not get his wish, but he has fled to his den at the bay." Liz sinks her chin to her chest.

"Where is this den?" Matt asks his gran.

"It is in Elf Land," she tells him. "King Gris has dug his den into the big hill in Elf Landing."

"King Gris is back in Elf Land!" Matt blasts. "He has a bad way of slipping off into Elf Land."

"What is that bad elf up to?" Twigs grunts.

"Grandma Deb got a lamp from the obelisk," Liz chips in. "I bet it can help us get rid of King Gris!"

Grandma Deb brings out the lamp. It glints in the sun just as the Spelling Pen does.

She hands it to Twigs.

"This is the Brass Lamp from the Red Obelisk!" he gasps.

He twists the lamp in his hands.

"Let us go to the huts," he tells them. "We must tell Mell and the rest of the clan that the Brass Lamp is in Elf Land. And so is King Gris."

Chapter 3
The Brass Lamp

The elf clan is glad that the Sun Kids are back in Elf Land.

At the huts, Liz and Matt hug Mell.

Twigs hands the lamp to Mell.

The elf clan gasps when the lamp glints.

"What does this lamp do?" asks an elf kid. "Where did you get it?"

"The Brass Lamp was in the Red Obelisk. The griffins and I hid it in the obelisk when I was a kid," Grandma Deb tells them.

"Can I check it out?" An elf in the back jumps in.

Mell nods, "But do not let it slip."

All in the elf clan wish to check out the lamp. They pass it from hand to hand.

"This Brass Lamp is an object of strength," Grandma Deb tells the elf clan. "The pen gets its spelling effects from this lamp. And so does the rest of the stunning objects in Elf Land."

"We must not let King Gris get his hands on it. If he does, he can limit the effects of the Spelling Pen," Twigs adds.

Matt clamps the Spelling Pen to his chest. "We must get the lamp to a spot where King Gris cannot get to."

"I must have the lamp back," Mell claps.

An elf in red hands it to Mell, but it slips!

"Oh, no!" Liz yells.

Matt jumps to grab the lamp, but it drops with a big thud.

Grandma Deb picks up the lamp in a rush and checks it.

It is still intact.

But the glass on the lamp has a big crack.

The lamp is dull and it does not glint.

Chapter 4
Crack In The Lamp

The elf in red is sad. His chin drops to his chest.

The elf clan stops. What will Twigs and Mell say?

Twigs gets upset. He cannot think of what to do next. He tells the elf clan to go back to their jobs.

As the clan drifts back to their huts, Twigs asks Matt, Liz and Grandma Deb to step into his hut to chat.

"This is a bad setback!" Twigs is still upset.

Matt asks, "Can the lamp still help the Spelling Pen if it has a crack?"

Grandma Deb is grim. "I do not think so. We must fix this lamp or ..."

"Or what?" Liz panics.

"Or the pen's spells will diminish. In the end, it will stop casting spells."

Liz is sad. "Then how can we go back to Mom and Dad? And how can we visit Elf Land when we must?"

"We can ask the griffins to help," Grandma Deb says. "The lamp was cast by griffin glass smiths when they were in Elf Land."

"What is a glass smith?" Liz asks.

Mell says, "A glass smith can craft things from glass. And griffins are the best glass smiths."

"Do you think they can fix the lamp?" Matt asks.

"Yes, I do," Grandma Deb nods.

"Where are the griffins?" asks Liz.

"They were in Ash Hill in Elf Land," says Twigs.

"We were in Ash Hill," Liz blasts with a thrill. "That was where King Gris dug out all the plants."

"When King Gris dug in Ash Hill, the griffins left Elf Land and went to Obelisk Land. Still, the king got wind of where the griffins were. Plus, his imps had a way to visit Obelisk Land. So, the griffins hid their crafts in Griffin Nest."

"Then we must go to Griffin Nest," Matt jumps up.

"Griffin Nest is up in the hills," Twigs says. "I think we must rest well until the trip."

"Will we go back to our land to rest?" Matt asks.

"No," says Grandma Deb. "We must limit the spells we cast with the Spelling Pen until we can fix the lamp."

Twigs brings them to the hut next to his.

"You can rest in this hut. I will be back when the sun is up."

Matt is still sad. "What if this is the end of the Spelling Pen."

Grandma Deb pats his hand. "It will be O.K. We will think of a plan."

She sets the lamp on the desk next to the bed. "The next day will be a big day. We must rest well."

Chapter 5
Trip To Griffin Nest

When the kids get up, they spot Grandma Deb sitting with a big map at the desk.

"What is that map?" Liz asks.

"It is the path to Griffin Nest," Grandma Deb says. "We will go on a raft and then trek the rest of the day. If we go fast, we will get to Griffin Nest by sunset."

"It will be fun to go to Griffin Nest," Liz claps. "And if the griffins can fix the lamp, then we can get rid of King Gris."

"Not if," Matt says, "WHEN they fix it!"

Just then, Mell and Twigs step into the hut.

The kids rush to them.

"Mell! Twigs!" Liz yells with a shrill. "We are off on a big quest to Griffin Nest!"

"Yes," Mell grins, "and we will go with you."

"The raft can fit six of us," Twigs says. "Pack the bags, then we will set off."

The kids pack their bags fast.

Liz packs snacks and drinks for the trip.

Matt packs the Spelling Pen.

Grandma Deb tucks the Brass Lamp in a thick fabric. Then she sets it in a box and packs it in her bag.

They go to the dock where Twigs and Mell are. They jump into the raft.

Matt and Liz drop the bags on the bench at the back of the raft. They sit next to Grandma Deb.

With the wind, the raft drifts fast.

"Tell us of griffins," Liz is snug next to her gran. "And the quest you had with them."

"You may think griffins are grim. But they are the best pals to have when you are in a pinch."

"How did you get the Spelling Pen when you were a kid?" Matt asks.

"I got it from my granddad when I was ten," Grandma Deb says.

"Do you still have that locket on your neck?" Matt asks.

She nods.

"What is in it?" Liz asks. "And what does it do?"

"A red relic is in it," she tells the kids.

Mell sits next to Liz. "Not to cut you off, but we must get off the raft."

"I will tell you what the relic is for when we end this mess," Grandma Deb tells the kids. "Until then, let us bring the Brass Lamp to the glass smiths."

Twigs stops the raft.

Mell jumps off and yanks the raft to a sandbank. They end up in a spot with lots of hills.

"Is this Griffin Nest?" the kids ask.

Chapter 6
End Of The Path

They are not at Griffin Nest yet.

"Next, we trek up this hill," Mell tells them. "Then we must pass a bit of grassland and a bunch of hills."

They grab the bags and go to the top of the hill.

The sun is hot!

Liz huffs and puffs. "Can we stop a bit? I must rest!"

Matt pants. "I want to rest as well."

Grandma Deb nods. "A rest can help us all. I think we are on the path, but I still want to check the map."

Mell and Twigs are glad to stop as well.

"I will grab a drink," Mell says.

They sit and rest on the thick grass next to the path and pass out cups of drinks.

"Thanks, Mell," Liz grins as she sips. "Yum! I did miss this hot plum drink."

Grandma Deb gets out the map and sets it on a flat rock.

Twigs helps her with the map. "Griffin Nest is to the west."

He checks the sun.

"The west is to the left," he adds.

"This is the path," Grandma Deb tells the rest.

Twigs nods. "The map says Griffin Nest is on top of that last hill."

"On we go," Grandma Deb packs up. "We must get to Griffin Nest by sunset."

The kids are fed up with trekking, but they do not nag. They wish to go to Griffin Nest to fix the lamp as fast as they can.

They plod on up the hill. They stop at the top of the next hill.

"This is the end of the path," says Grandma Deb in shock.

Twigs checks the sun and the hill where Griffin Nest is.

There is no way to get to Griffin Nest unless they have wings.

Chapter 7
The Griffins

Grandma Deb brings out the map. "Liz, set your hand on the map so it will not drift off in the wind."

Liz grips the map, but a bug stings her leg. She lets her hand off the map to smash it.

Just then, the wind picks up. A quick gust lifts the map off the rock.

Liz gasps.

Twigs and Mell jump to grab the map, but they cannot.

The wind sends the map to Griffin Nest off a big cliff.

"Matt! Liz! Stop!" yells Grandma Deb as the kids run for the map. "Do not go off the cliff."

Matt and Liz skid to a stop.

"What will we do with no map?" Liz asks. "How will we get to Griffin Nest?"

Grandma Deb inspects the cliff.

It is a big drop.

"Not much we can do. This is, in fact, the end of the path."

Then there is a flap of wings. Mell spots an object.

"What is that?" he yelps as he ducks.

A big griffin lands with a thud in front of them on the clifftop. Its big wings block the path.

The big griffin is grim.

"Stop! Drop the stuff in your hands, then lift them up."

Six griffins land by the bunch from Elf Land so they cannot run off.

Matt, Liz, Grandma Deb, Mell and Twigs stand with their hands up as the griffin steps up to them.

"We wish the griffins well," Liz says.

"Hush!" The big griffin extends his wings.

"You can trust us," Grandma Deb adds. "Bring me to Flint. I must chat with him."

The griffins gasp.

The big griffin squints, "You ask for Flint?"

Grandma Deb says, "Yes. I am Deb. I met Flint in Elf Land when I was a kid."

"Sun Kid Deb?" gasps a griffin from the back.

Chapter 8
Griffin Nest

Grandma Deb nods. "Matt and Liz are my grandkids. They are Sun Kids as well. Mell and Twigs are pals from Elf Land."

The big griffin says, "I am Chip. I think Flint will wish to chat with you as well. But you cannot trek up to Griffin Nest. You must get up on our backs."

Chip bends and Grandma Deb gets on his back.

Matt and Liz hop on a big griffin.

The kids grasp on and pray they do not fall off.

Mell and Twigs sit on the back of a black griffin.

"Let us go to Griffin Nest," Chip says. "Hang on!"

The griffins lift off fast and swift.

They pass a lot of hills and Matt can tell there is no way to get to Griffin Nest with no wings.

At last, the griffins land on the top of the last hill.

This is Griffin Nest.

"We must go and tell Flint and the rest of the griffins that Sun Kid Deb is in Griffin Nest."

The griffins lift off.

The kids sit on a big, flat rock slab.

"Well," Mell says. "Do you think the griffins will help us or is this a big trap?"

"They will help us," Grandma Deb tells them.

In a snap, the griffins are back.

The kids stand up when they land.

A big griffin is in front of the bunch.

"Sun Kid Deb! Is that you?" he asks with a big grin. "Last we met, you were just a kid."

Grandma Deb steps up to him. "Flint! And you are still just as you were back then."

"Oh, stop that!" Flint grins. "And who is visiting us with you?" he asks.

"Liz and Matt are my grandkids," she tells the griffin.

"I expect they are Sun Kids as well," says Flint.

"Yes, for a fact," Grandma Deb nods.

Flint nods back with a grin.

"This is Mell and this is Twigs. They are from Elf Land," she adds.

"I miss Elf Land so much!" Flint taps his hand on his chin. "It was a land of bliss, not just for the griffins but for all. I wish things to go back to how they were."

"So does the elf clan," Mell nods.

"Well, Sun Kid Deb's pals are our pals as well," Flint tells them. Then he asks, "What brings you back to us? A visit to Griffin Nest is a hint that not all is well."

Grandma Deb nods. "Yes, there is a big setback. Things are bad. King Gris has run off!"

Then she brings out the Brass Lamp from her bag.

"Is that the Brass Lamp we hid in the Red Obelisk?" Flint gasps in shock.

"Yes," Grandma Deb nods. "And it has a big crack!"

Chapter 9
The Griffin Sand

Flint inspects the crack in the glass.

"I will get the best glass smiths in Griffin Nest on the job."

"Then you can fix this lamp!" Matt claps with a big grin.

"Well," says Flint, "we do have the best shot at fixing it."

Matt winks at Liz.

"We must get a lot of logs for the big kiln to melt the sand and fix the glass on the Brass Lamp." Flint directs the griffins.

"We have a stack of logs at the shed. But we must add a lot of logs to the stack," a griffin steps up. "The kiln must get hot."

"What can I do?" Liz asks to help.

"Can you chop logs with an ax?" Flint asks.

"No," Liz shrugs.

"But I can!" Matt says. "I can swing an ax."

"Fantastic, Matt," Flint claps. "Then, Liz, you can brush the ash out of the kiln."

Matt and Liz jump up. They will do the best they can to help.

Twigs and Mell go with the griffins to bring lots of logs.

Matt chops the logs from the shed with an ax.

Liz and Grandma Deb brush the ash off of the kiln until not a speck is left.

A griffin kid digs pink sand out of the sandpit and sifts it into a big bucket.

Matt checks the sand in the pit. "Is this the sand the glass smiths will melt to get the glass?"

He runs his hand in the sand.

"Yes," the griffin kid nods. "This is the griffin sand."

Matt thinks the pink glint in the sand is dazzling.

The griffin kid adds, "When this sand melts, we get the best glass."

"But there is no pink tint in the glass of the Brass Lamp." Matt rubs the sand off his hands. "Will it still do the job?"

The griffin kid shrugs. "This is the sand we have in Griffin Nest."

Chapter 10
A Big Flop

A bunch of glass smiths bring buckets of sand to the kiln. They cram the kiln with the logs Matt had split. Then they lock it up.

When the kiln gets red hot with the logs, the glass smiths unlock the kiln and set in the griffin sand.

The kids step up to check how the sand melts.

It is hot at the kiln. Flint tells them they must stand back.

"This is not a job for kids," he adds.

Matt and Liz step back.

"When will the sand melt?" Liz asks. "Will it be quick?"

"It will be a bit," Flint says. "If you wish, you can visit the craft shop and check out lots of fun crafts."

Matt and Liz clap with a thrill.

Flint grins. "Let us check what we have in stock."

He brings the kids to the craft shop. The shop has so much in it.

He tells the kids he must check on the glass smiths and steps out of the shop.

The kids inspect all the crafts.

They go to a shelf that has glass pots, lamps and bulbs.

"Check this out," Matt tugs at Liz. "Can you spot the pink flecks in the glass craft?"

Liz picks up a glass pot. "Yes. They all have pink specks in them from the sand."

"Yes! The griffin sand has a pink tint," Matt says. "But I do not think the glass in the Brass Lamp has pink flecks."

"I did not inspect the lamp that much," Liz shrugs. "I expect it is not a big thing. The griffins are the best glass smiths. I trust them to do this well."

"So do I," Matt insists. "But still, there are no pink flecks in the lamp."

He brings out the Spelling Pen from his pocket. He can tell that the pen's glints are diminishing bit by bit. As it does, so will the Spelling Pen's effects. Just then, Grandma Deb steps in the craft shop.

"Did you say pink sand?" she gasps. "They cannot mix pink sand into the glass of the Brass Lamp! If they do…"

There is a big bang!

Chapter 11
A Web Of Cracks

The glass crafts fall off the shelf with a crash.

"What was that?" Matt yells in shock.

Grandma Deb grabs Matt's and Liz's hands as they run out.

Lots of griffins rush to the kiln.

Flint yells, "Stop melting the sand! Rub it off the lamp!"

Flint spots Grandma Deb. He runs to her.

"This is a big setback," he tells her. "When we set the griffin sand on the lamp, there was a flash."

Then he yells. "Bring me the Brass Lamp, Chip."

Flint inspects the lamp. It is still hot.

The glass on the lamp has a web of cracks.

"Why did the sand not fix the lamp?" Liz grunts.

Flint twists the lamp in his hand. "The griffin sand did not blend in with the glass on the Brass Lamp."

"Why is that?" Liz asks.

"It must be the pink sand," Grandma Deb tells them.

Matt jumps in the chat, "The griffin sand has pink flecks. But the glass on the lamp has no pink in it."

"Why did I not think of that?" Flint stomps.

"Stop the kiln," Chip yells at the glass smiths.

"No, do not stop it," Grandma Deb yells back. "The lamp must be kept hot or the cracks will split."

Matt brings out the Spelling Pen. The pen is dull with no glints.

He clicks the pen, but it cannot do a thing. He sticks the pen in his backpack.

Matt yelps, "The Spelling Pen has no..."

Flint grabs the pen from Matt.

"We are out of luck," he squints.

"What are you telling us?" Matt snaps at the griffin.

Mell and Twigs gasp. "So much is at risk!"

"What can we do?" Liz panics. "We cannot let the Spelling Pen crash."

"We must fix the Brass Lamp fast," Matt blasts.

Chapter 12
Glass Smith's Script

The glass smiths bring the kiln down to 750^0F.

They rub the pink melt off the glass as much as they can. Then they set the lamp back in the kiln.

"What can we do next?" Matt asks.

"Bring the Glass Smith's Script," Flint tells the griffins. "We must check what the griffins had in the sand mix in the past when crafting the Brass Lamp!"

Chip runs in a flash.

"What is the Glass Smith's Script?" Liz asks.

"It is a set of texts that tell how to craft things from glass," Flint says.

"And do you think the Brass Lamp is in this script?" Matt asks.

"Yes," Flint nods. "Griffin glass smiths log all they craft. So it must be in the script."

Chip sprints back with the script in his hand.

"I got the script!" he yells as he hands it to Flint.

"Brass Lamp… Brass Lamp…" Flint scans the text. "Got it! It instructs how to melt the sand for the glass in the lamp."

"Black silk and red sand," he grunts. "That is what is in the glass of the Brass Lamp."

Grandma Deb nods. "Shreds of black silk add strength to the glass.

We must blend a bit of black silk in the red sand to fix the lamp."

Chip taps his chin. "So we must get black silk and red sand."

"In fact, the script says the sand will crack the lamp if we do not add the black silk to it." Flint is grim. "And that is just what it did!"

"What is black silk?" Liz asks.

"It is strips of the stem of a plant," Flint says.

"What plant is that?" Matt asks.

"It is Satin Blush," Chip says.

"How much must we get?" Twigs asks.

"Not much," says Grandma Deb. "A shred of the stem and a cup of red sand will do the trick. Just cut a bit of the stem. Do not dig the Satin Blush out. That will kill the plant."

"And the red sand?" Matt asks. "Where will we get that?"

"The sand next to the Satin Blush plant shifts from tan to red," Twigs jumps in the chat. "So if we get to the plant, we can get the red sand as well."

"Where can we get this Satin Blush?" Liz asks.

"Not in Griffin Nest," Chip shrugs.

"Well, where then?" Matt asks.

Flint says, "It is on Ash Hill in Elf Land."

Chapter 13
The Rock In The Locket

"So what is next?" asks Matt.

"I will go to Ash Hill with Mell," Twigs tells Matt.

"We will go with you," a big griffin jumps in.

The griffin next to him nods.

Flint tells them to get back to Griffin Nest by sunset.

Twigs and Mell get on the griffins and off they go.

"Sun Kid Deb," Flint grabs her hand. "You must stay in Griffin Nest and help the glass smiths with the lamp. And Chip, you must go to Obelisk Land to check for Satin Blush."

"Can we go with Chip?" the kids ask Grandma Deb.

Grandma Deb nods.

"Matt, do you have the Spelling Pen on you?" she asks.

"No," he shrugs.

Liz brings out the pen from his bag and hands it to Matt.

"But it does not cast spells!" He hands the dull pen back to Liz.

"You must bring it with you," Grandma Deb insists. "Trust me. You must have it on you."

Matt nods.

He sticks the pen in his jacket pocket and the kids get on Chip's back. The griffin lifts off with the kids.

Flint taps Grandma Deb on her chest.

"When you got the Brass Lamp out of the Red Obelisk, did you get the wishing rock as well?" Flint asks.

"Yes." Grandma Deb brings her hand to her neck. "It is in my locket."

"Did you tell Matt and Liz what it can do?" Flint squints.

"Not yet." Grandma Deb says. "What if there is no Satin Blush left in Ash Hill or Obelisk Land?"

"Then all bets will be off," Flint shrugs in a sad way. "I do not have to tell you where the last spot is, do I?"

"No, you do not." Grandma Deb cuts him off. "But I do not want to think of a trip to Elf Landing."

Chapter 14
The Quicksand

Chip drifts on top of the hill where the Red Obelisk was.

They do not spot a drop of red sand at all.

Chip lands next to a sandbank. "Let us dig in this spot."

The kids jump off.

They bring out a pickax from the backpack.

Liz jumps in the sand.

Chip says, "Liz, do not dig in that spot in the midst of the sand. Stick to the bank."

"I think there may be red sand in this spot," Liz insists.

She hefts her pickax and digs. Matt digs as well. But the sand is not red. He stops when Liz yells for help.

Liz's leg gets stuck and she sinks in the sand.

"Help! Help! Help!" she yells.

Liz is stuck in quicksand!

She sinks as the sand sucks in her legs.

Liz is frantic!

"Do not panic!" Chip yells. "If you do, you will sink fast!"

But Liz does panic. She sinks to her hips, still yelling.

"Liz, stop flapping!" Matt blasts. "If you are still, then you will stop sinking."

Liz sobs, but she stops flapping.

"What is this?" asks Matt.

"It is quicksand. The sand in the pit is wet and sucks her in," Chip says as he grabs a big log. "Help me, Matt. We must bring this to Liz."

Matt and Chip drag the thick branch to her.

"Grab this," Chip casts the branch to Liz. "Do not let go!"

She clings to the log.

Matt and Flint drag the branch back. They step back bit by bit until Liz is at the brink of the sandbank.

They clench Liz's hands. And at last, she is out.

"Le... Le... Let us just ch… check for the plant." Liz is shaking and dripping wet.

"We must go back to Griffin Nest," Chip says. "You are wet and it is sunset."

The kids jump on Chip's back, but then Matt pats his pants' pockets.

"Where is the Spelling Pen?" he gasps.

Chapter 15

Hunt For The Spelling Pen

Matt panics. "Did it drop in the quicksand?"

He jumps off Chip's back and runs back to the sandbank.

Liz gets off as well.

"I think it fell when Chip and I were dragging you out of the quicksand." Matt panics.

He still pats his back pockets.

"This is such a mess!" he stomps.

They rush to check the sand.

The kids dig in with sticks and the pickax.

They brush the sand back as much as they can.

But the pen is not there.

"Matt, what is that?" Liz squints.

"What?" Matt asks.

"What is that st... sticking out of your jacket pock... pocket?" Liz is still shaking.

Matt pats his pocket. He gets all red as he yanks out the Spelling Pen.

"It... it... was in your jack... jacket!"

Matt hugs Liz. "I was quick to panic. Glad we still have the pen."

He tucks the pen in and zips his pocket.

"Let us go," Chip says. "We must get Liz a hot drink and a snug blanket."

They hop on Chip's back and go back to the nest.

Chapter 16
The Last Spot

Back at the nest, Mell, Twigs and the griffins are back from Ash Hill.

"If they are back this fast, it cannot be O.K.," Grandma Deb thinks.

Chip and the kids are the last to get back.

Chip hands Liz off to Grandma Deb and tells her of Liz's fall into quicksand. He asks a griffin to get Liz a blanket and mix a hot drink.

"Well?" Flint asks Mell and Twigs. "Did you get the red sand and black silk?"

"No. Not a plant or a shrub is left on Ash Hill," Mell tells Flint.

"It is just rocks and dust," Twigs adds. "There is no Satin Blush left at all."

"The spell of the pen is crumbling," Mell squints. "We must fix the Brass Lamp or the land will go back to how it was when King Gris was digging. It will be the end of Elf Land!"

Flint is sad. "And you, Chip?"

"Not a hint of a Satin Blush plant in Obelisk Land," Chip shrugs.

"That cannot be the last spot to get this plant," Liz insists.

"There is still a spot where we can get the red sand and black silk," Flint says.

The kids grin.

"And we must go there if you wish to fix the lamp," he adds.

"Where?" Matt asks.

"It is at Elf Landing."

"Elf Landing!" Matt blasts. "You must be kidding!"

"I wish I was," Flint tells Matt. "That is where King's Den is, but we must go there."

Chapter 17
The Black Silk

"The Satin Blush is in Elf Landing where King Gris is," Liz stomps. "What a big mess!"

She still hugs the hot cup of drink in her hand.

Matt is upset. "There must be a spot to get this plant that is not next to his den."

"This is the last spot," Grandma Deb hugs Matt.

"Not a bit of Satin Blush was left in Ash Hill or Obelisk Land. Elf Landing is the last spot," Flint pats Matt on the back.

"Why did the lamp had to have the red sand and the black silk in it?" Matt grunts.

"We will go on the hunt," Chip says. "On your wings, Griffins!"

"Not so fast," Flint stops them. "We cannot just jump into this mess with no plan. Let us plot what to do."

Grandma Deb says, "If King Gris is still at his den, we cannot just pop up at Elf Landing. We will not have the help of the Spelling Pen until we fix the Brass Lamp. It is a big risk to let him spot us by his den."

Twigs nods. "We must slip in Elf Landing to get the black silk and red sand. Then we get out as fast as we can."

"King Gris must not spot us," Mell adds. "If we stick to the hilltop, we can slip in and out fast. When we have the pen's spells back, we can go back for him."

"We can do that," Chip claps.

Flint nods. "I think that Twigs and Mell must go to Elf Landing, as well as Chip and I."

He hands the Griffin Smith's Script to Grandma Deb.

"Check all of it. If we cannot get the black silk and red sand, then you must…"

Grandma Deb stops Flint.

"You will get back with the silk and the sand. But I will check the script as a backup."

Chapter 18
The Big Plan

"Can Matt and I go as well?" Liz asks. "We can help in the hunt."

"You must ask Sun Kid Deb," Flint tells her.

Grandma Deb nods. "You can go with Flint."

Liz grins and claps. She is glad they get to go on this quest. But Matt is not as glad as Liz is.

"I do wish to go on the quest," Matt tells Grandma Deb. "But I cannot cast spells with the Spelling Pen. What if we run into King Gris? What will we do then?"

Grandma Deb sits Matt on a log. She sits next to him.

"You do not have the pen's spells, but you have still got your wits. You can win on this quest. You will get the black silk and the red sand," she insists.

Matt nods with a half grin.

"Bring the pen with you to Elf Landing. So you have it on you when we fix the Brass Lamp."

Matt shrugs.

Grandma Deb hugs him. "We are the Sun Kids. We will fix the Brass Lamp. We will bring back the spells of the Spelling Pen!"

Flint says, "We must rest. We will have a big day at Elf Landing."

As the rest drift off to go to bed, Chip taps Flint on the back. "Do you think it is best to bring Matt and Liz with us to Elf Landing? I bet King Gris is in his den."

Flint says, "We must have Sun Kids with us. They think quick and spot things the rest of us do not."

"They are just kids and they will risk our plans," Chip insists.

"They are our best shot at fixing this lamp and bring bliss back to Elf Land. And we will be there to help them."

Chapter 19

Elf Landing

The sun is up.

This is the day they will visit Elf Landing. Will they run into King Gris?

Matt pats his jacket pocket. The Spelling Pen does not cast spells but Matt is still glad to have the pen with him.

The pickax is still in the backpack from the trip to Obelisk Land.

Flint says, "Jump on my back and we will set off."

Matt and Twigs sit on Flint's back. Liz and Mell get on Chip.

They set off for Elf Landing.

The griffins land on the hilltop and the kids get off.

"Quick," Flint tells the rest. "Let us check for Satin Blush and red sand. Then we must get out of Elf Landing as fast as we can."

Mell, Twigs and Matt all get out the pickax. They dig on the hilltop, but there is no red sand.

Flint, Chip and Liz shift to a spot on the tip top of the hill.

They check the summit for Satin Blush.

Then, Liz spots a plant.

"This must be it," she thinks and bends in the grass.

"Is this Satin Blush?" she asks Flint.

Flint steps up and sniffs the plant. "No, it is not."

Just then, Matt swings the pickax in the sand. A stash of red sand crops up!

"Check this out. This sand is red," he yells as he digs with his hands.

"If there is red sand, a Satin Blush must be on this hill," Chip inspects the hilltop.

Mell and Twigs rush to fill up the buckets.

"How much must we get?" they ask.

"Just fill the buckets," Flint tells them. "Let us bring as much as we can back to Griffin Nest."

Liz spots a pit next to the red sand.

"What is this?" she yells.

Flint is mad. "That cannot be!"

"Where is the plant?" Mell panics.

Matt spots a track of red sand down the hill.

"I think a Satin Blush plant was at this spot, but King Gris dug it out."

"If we cannot get to it fast, it will go extinct," Twigs gasps. "Then we cannot fix the lamp!"

Matt spots the plant next to the King's Den at the bed of the hill.

"I will rush to the den and get the plant," Matt tells the griffins. "Be set to run off when I am back. We must get out Elf Landing fast."

"Matt, do not…" Flint blasts.

But Matt runs off.

Bits of rocks fall down the hill as Matt sprints as fast as he can.

With that, King Gris can tell it is a visit he will not be fond of. But the king does not rush. He thinks his trap will get them.

Chapter 20

The Trap

In a blink, Matt is down by the den next to the Satin Blush plant.

He cuts a bit of the stem. Then he spots buds and a thin branch that fell off next to the plant. The plant is fading.

Plus, the sand next to the Satin Blush is not that red. Matt can tell the plant will not last at this spot. So he picks up the plant and sets it in his pocket.

Then he runs up the hill as fast as he can.

"We must get out of Elf Landing!" he yells. "I got the black silk!"

As Matt sprints up to Flint, he slips. In a blink, the sand shifts and a big net pops up.

"It is a trap!" Liz yells.

Chip grabs Liz's hand and jumps back, dragging her with him. He slips flat on his back and shrills as his wings twist back.

The net springs up and grabs up Matt, Twigs, Mell and Flint.

"Oh, no!" Matt yells.

The net hangs from a big branch, and they are stuck in it!

"Jot with the Spelling Pen?" Liz blasts. "Check if it can cast a spell!"

Matt yanks the pen from his pocket and jots on his pad: 'Get us out of the net.'

But the pen still will not glint.

"The Spelling Pen has no effect," Matt yells back.

Flint says, "Liz. Chip. You must get the black silk and the red sand back to Griffin Nest."

"No!" Liz sobs. "I cannot go back when Matt is stuck in a trap in Elf Landing. I cannot just run off."

"You must help the glass smiths fix the lamp. Then we have a shot at getting out of this trap." Flint insists.

"Liz, you are the last shot we have," Matt says. "You and Chip must bring the black silk and red sand to Griffin Nest. You must go back to Grandma Deb."

Liz sniffs. "Matt, Chip and I will do the best we can."

Chapter 21
Chip's Wing

Chip sets the lids on the buckets so the sand will not spill.

Matt hands the black silk and Satin Blush to Liz. "You must plant the Satin Blush in Griffin Nest out of King Gris's grasp."

Liz sets them in her pocket. She grabs the buckets of red sand. Then she hops on Chip's back.

But Chip cannot lift his wing.

"My wing is not well." He grabs his left wing. "I cannot lift up with the buckets and you on my back."

Liz and Chip drag the buckets and slog on step by step.

In a bit, Liz tells Chip, "You must rest."

"I will rest when we get back to Griffin Nest," Chip plods on.

But he can tell that they cannot bring all this sand to Griffin Nest.

"We must drop the sand," he pants.

"Drop the sand?" Liz says in shock.

"We must limit the sand we bring," Chip nods. "Let us just bring the big bucket."

They go on for a bit. But the big bucket is still a lot for them to drag.

"If we go this fast, we will not get to Griffin Nest by sunset." Liz is grim.

"This is the best we can do. I think we just bring what we must. Can you tell how much?"

"Grandma Deb did say it was a cup of sand." Liz taps her chin.

"That is not much," Chip grins.

He tilts the big bucket and spills out half the sand.

"This will do." He hands the bucket to Liz. "Get on my back. I can lift off with this much."

Liz hugs the griffin's neck. "Get us back as fast as you can. I cannot think what King Gris will do if he gets his hands on Matt and the rest."

Chip flaps as fast as he can. They do not rest a bit.

It is dim when they get to Griffin Nest.

Chapter 22

Stuck In The Net

Back at Elf Landing, the net hangs from the big branch.

Matt, Flint, Mell and Twigs are still stuck in it.

"Can we cut this net?" Matt asks.

"I do not have the ax. It is in that pit," Twigs grunts.

"The string is thick," Mell says. "I cannot snap it with my hands."

"Can we get the net to fall off the branch?" Matt asks.

They rock the net to get it to fall. The net swings, but it will not fall. It is still stuck on the branch.

Matt dips his hand into his pocket for the Spelling Pen. He brings the pen out and bangs it on his hip.

Then he jots: 'Go back to Griffin Nest.'

Not a flash.

He jots: 'Get us out of this trap.'

No gust of wind.

He jots: 'Bring the pen's spells back.'

Not a thing.

"I wish I was out of this net!" he grunts.

The sun sets. It gets dim, then black. They think they will be stuck in the net until King Gris gets to them.

"Do you think Liz and Chip got to Griffin Nest yet?" Matt asks.

"If they did not stop, they must be back," Flint says.

Matt says, "They will do the best they can."

"I trust them to bring the red sand and black silk back to the glass smiths," Flint tells them.

Just then, there is a yell. "What gift is there for me in this net?"

An elf pops up the hill and stands in front of them.

It is King Gris!

Chapter 23
King Gris Is Back

"Ha, ha!" King Gris taps his chin. "A Sun Kid got stuck in my trap!"

Mell and Twigs gasp.

King Gris stands next to the branch where the net hangs.

"A Sun Kid and his elf pals," King Gris claps. "And a griffin as well! You did your best to block my plans. And where did it get you? Stuck in my net."

Matt taps the pen to his chest.

It still does not glint.

"What will I do with you?" King Gris yells with a shrill. "Well, you can hand me that Spelling Pen. You cannot trick me with it!"

"I will not hand the pen to you," Matt yells back.

He will not tell King Gris that the pen has no effect until the griffins fix the Brass Lamp.

"We will get out of this net fast," he blasts.

"Well, I am the King of Elf Land." King Gris stomps. "And you do as I say!"

Matt clicks the Spelling Pen. Still not a glint!

"Plus, I wish to win and, at last, I have a shot." King Gris grins. "And if I crush the pen, then you cannot stop me, SunKid!"

"If you crush the pen, you will win. But you will be the king of a land of rocks and dust," Mell blasts. "Is that what you wish?"

"Hush!" King Gris squints.

He stands in front of the net. He taps his chin and thinks. But what will he do?

"For me to win," the king grins, "I will crush that pen into dust!"

He jumps to grab the pen from Matt. But Matt lifts the pen and King Gris cannot get it.

"Let me have it!" King Gris grunts.

Mell slaps King Gris's hand and the elf king yelps.

Matt spins the Spelling Pen in his hand.

In a blink, the pen glints.

Chapter 24

Spelling Pen Glints

"Flint! I think Liz and Chip did it!" Matt blasts with a thrill.

The glints from the Spelling Pen fill Elf Landing.

Matt grabs the pad from his pocket.

He jots: 'Get us out of the net.'

In a flash, the net splits in half and they drop with a thud.

"The Spelling Pen is back!" Twigs yells.

"Thank you, Liz and Chip," Matt grins.

He stands up fast and helps the rest get up as well. They must get out of Elf Landing as fast as they can.

Still, they must get rid of King Gris as well.

"What do you think, Flint?" he asks. "Can we bust King Gris or do we just get back to Griffin Nest fast?"

"I say back to Griffin Nest." Flint is blunt.

Matt nods. "Let us not risk it. Back we go!"

"We will be back for King Gris!" Mell winks at Matt.

"Hop on my back," Flint yells.

"All of us?" Twigs gasps.

"I got a plan!" Matt taps the Spelling Pen on his hand.

The pen glints.

Mell, Twigs, Flint and Matt... They all glint.

Matt jots: 'Get us back to Griffin Nest.'

There is a rush of wind.

Then a big flash.

King Gris stamps and yells. "No! No! No!"

In a quick flash, Matt and his pals vanish from Elf Landing.

Chapter 25
Back At Griffin Nest

Matt, Twigs, Mell and Flint end up in front of the kiln in Griffin Nest.

They are all glad to be back.

The griffins rush to them, led by Liz.

"You did it!" she yells.

The Spelling Pen still glints in Matt's hand.

Matt grins. "No, it was you! You got the black silk and the red sand to the griffins! Tell me how you did it!"

Liz says, "Chip and I had to drag the buckets of sand. We did not stop to rest until we got back. On the way, we had to dump a lot of the sand. But we got what we had to the glass smiths. Then the glass smiths did the rest."

"Where is the Brass Lamp?" Flint asks.

A glass smith says, "Sun Kid Deb has it. She is in the craft shop."

Matt, Chip and Liz go to the craft shop.

Grandma Deb runs up to them.

"Fantastic job, Matt," she hugs him.

Matt grins. "It was thanks to Liz that we fled from King Gris's trap."

Flint checks the Brass Lamp. "The glass smiths did a fantastic job," he says. "You cannot tell the glass had a crack in it."

"Yes! The lamp and the Spelling Pen are back at last," Matt adds. "But

King Gris is still in Elf Land. We still did not stop his plans."

"Not yet," Flint says. "But with the Spelling Pen back, you will stop him."

"What will we do with the lamp?" Liz asks.

"I did discuss this with Flint. We think it is best if the lamp stays in Griffin Nest." Grandma Deb says.

The kids are glad for that. They do not wish King Gris to get his hands on the lamp.

"Plus, I have a big thing to tell you." Grandma Deb sits the kids on a big log. "I must tell you what is in my locket so you can go on the next quest."

You can download full color

CERTIFICATE OF ACCOMPLISHMENT
and
CERTIFICATE OF COMPLETION

on our website

SIMPLEWORDSBOOKS.COM

Certificate of Accomplishment

This certificate is awarded to

_____

for successful completion of

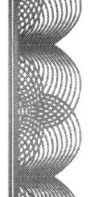

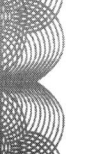

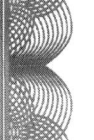

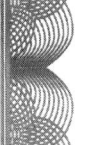

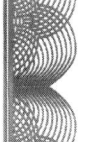

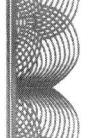

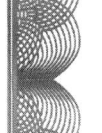

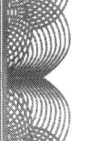

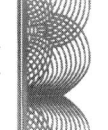

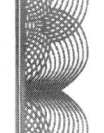

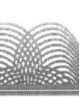

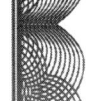

Spelling Pen Brass Lamp

_____   _____
Signature   Date

SIMPLE WORDS

SPELLING PEN
BRASS LAMP
WORD LIST

#	Word	Count	#	Word	Count	#	Word	Count
1	a	174	26	bay	1	51	brings	13
2	add	3	27	be	28	52	brink	1
3	adds	11	28	bed	3	53	brush	3
4	all	21	29	bench	1	54	bucket	5
5	am	4	30	bends	2	55	buckets	8
6	an	11	31	best	15	56	buds	1
7	and	184	32	bet	3	57	bug	1
8	are	45	33	bets	1	58	bulbs	1
9	as	64	34	big	44	59	bunch	5
10	ash	11	35	bit	15	60	bust	1
11	ask	6	36	bits	1	61	but	49
12	asks	48	37	black	20	62	by	12
13	at	37	38	blanket	2	63	can	68
14	ax	4	39	blasts	10	64	cannot	29
15	back	85	40	blend	2	65	cast	7
16	backpack	3	41	blink	3	66	casting	1
17	backs	1	42	bliss	2	67	casts	2
18	backup	1	43	block	2	68	chat	5
19	bad	5	44	blunt	1	69	check	19
20	bag	3	45	blush	19	70	checks	5
21	bags	4	46	box	1	71	chest	5
22	bang	1	47	brags	1	72	chin	7
23	bangs	1	48	branch	9	73	Chip	56
24	bank	1	49	brass	28	74	chips	1
25	basilisk	8	50	bring	23	75	chop	1

#	Word	Count	#	Word	Count	#	Word	Count
76	chops	1	101	day	5	126	dripping	1
77	clamps	1	102	dazzling	1	127	drop	8
78	clan	13	103	Deb	81	128	drops	2
79	clap	1	104	den	11	129	ducks	1
80	claps	7	105	desk	2	130	dug	5
81	clench	1	106	did	32	131	dull	3
82	clicks	2	107	dig	5	132	dump	1
83	cliff	3	108	digging	1	133	dust	3
84	clifftop	1	109	digs	4	134	effect	2
85	clings	1	110	dim	2	135	effects	3
86	crack	6	111	diminish	1	136	elf	79
87	cracks	2	112	diminishing	1	137	end	9
88	craft	9	113	dips	1	138	expect	2
89	crafting	1	114	directs	1	139	extends	1
90	crafts	4	115	discuss	1	140	extinct	1
91	cram	1	116	do	67	141	fabric	1
92	crash	2	117	dock	1	142	fact	5
93	crops	1	118	does	13	143	fading	1
94	crumbling	1	119	down	4	144	fall	7
95	crush	3	120	drag	5	145	fantastic	3
96	cup	3	121	dragging	2	146	fast	23
97	cups	1	122	drift	2	147	fed	1
98	cut	3	123	drifts	3	148	fell	2
99	cuts	2	124	drink	5	149	fill	3
100	dad	1	125	drinks	2	150	fills	3

#	Word	Count
151	fit	1
152	fix	19
153	fixing	2
154	flap	1
155	flapping	2
156	flaps	1
157	flash	7
158	flat	3
159	flecks	4
160	fled	2
161	Flint	81
162	fog	1
163	fond	1
164	for	25
165	frantic	1
166	from	35
167	front	6
168	fun	2
169	gasp	3
170	gasps	11
171	get	75
172	gets	12
173	getting	1
174	gift	4
175	glad	9

#	Word	Count
176	glass	45
177	glint	6
178	glints	9
179	go	49
180	goblins	1
181	got	20
182	grab	6
183	grabs	9
184	gran	2
185	granddad	1
186	grandkids	2
187	grandma	73
188	grasp	3
189	grass	2
190	grassland	1
191	griffin	76
192	griffins	36
193	grim	5
194	grin	5
195	grins	11
196	grips	1
197	Gris	49
198	grunts	8
199	gust	2
200	ha	2

#	Word	Count
201	had	10
202	half	3
203	hand	20
204	hands	23
205	hang	1
206	hangs	3
207	has	18
208	have	30
209	he	92
210	hefts	1
211	help	20
212	helps	2
213	her	26
214	hid	6
215	hill	25
216	hills	4
217	hilltop	4
218	him	19
219	hint	2
220	hip	1
221	hips	1
222	his	64
223	hop	3
224	hops	1
225	hot	10

#	Word	Count
226	how	14
227	huffs	1
228	hug	1
229	hugs	6
230	hunt	2
231	hush	2
232	hut	4
233	huts	4
234	I	91
235	if	29
236	imps	2
237	in	159
238	insists	8
239	inspect	2
240	inspects	4
241	instructs	1
242	intact	1
243	into	15
244	is	170
245	it	121
246	its	2
247	jack	1
248	jacket	4
249	job	5
250	jobs	1

#	Word	Count
251	jot	1
252	jots	8
253	jump	7
254	jumps	12
255	just	25
256	kept	1
257	kid	20
258	kidding	1
259	kids	36
260	kill	1
261	kiln	14
262	king	58
263	Krig	8
264	lamp	75
265	lamps	1
266	land	55
267	landing	22
268	lands	2
269	last	15
270	led	2
271	left	11
272	leg	2
273	legs	1
274	let	18
275	lets	1

#	Word	Count
276	lids	1
277	lift	6
278	lifts	3
279	limit	3
280	link	1
281	Liz	119
282	lock	1
283	locket	3
284	log	5
285	logs	8
286	lot	5
287	lots	4
288	luck	1
289	mad	1
290	map	15
291	mass	1
292	Matt	156
293	may	2
294	me	12
295	Mell	50
296	melt	5
297	melting	1
298	melts	2
299	mess	4
300	met	2

#	Word	Count	#	Word	Count	#	Word	Count
301	midst	1	326	our	5	351	plods	1
302	miss	2	327	out	47	352	plot	2
303	mist	1	328	pack	2	353	plum	1
304	mix	3	329	packs	4	354	plus	4
305	mom	1	330	pad	2	355	pock	1
306	much	15	331	pals	6	356	pocket	11
307	must	72	332	panic	3	357	pockets	2
308	my	14	333	panics	5	358	pop	1
309	nag	1	334	pants	3	359	pops	2
310	neck	3	335	pass	4	360	pot	1
311	nest	46	336	past	1	361	pots	1
312	net	18	337	path	8	362	pray	1
313	next	27	338	pats	6	363	puffs	1
314	no	31	339	pen	70	364	quest	8
315	nods	25	340	pickax	6	365	quests	1
316	not	80	341	picks	4	366	quick	6
317	O.K.	2	342	pinch	1	367	quicksand	5
318	obelisk	25	343	pink	14	368	raft	8
319	object	2	344	pit	4	369	ran	1
320	objects	1	345	plan	3	370	red	44
321	of	115	346	planning	1	371	relic	2
322	off	39	347	plans	4	372	rest	25
323	oh	3	348	plant	22	373	rid	5
324	on	78	349	plants	1	374	risk	6
325	or	10	350	plod	1	375	rock	5

#	Word	Count
376	rocks	3
377	rub	2
378	rubs	1
379	run	9
380	runs	7
381	rush	9
382	sad	5
383	sand	77
384	sandbank	4
385	sandpit	1
386	sank	1
387	satin	19
388	say	5
389	says	55
390	scans	1
391	script	9
392	sends	1
393	set	9
394	setback	3
395	sets	7
396	shaking	2
397	she	38
398	shed	2
399	shelf	2
400	shift	1

#	Word	Count
401	shifts	2
402	shock	4
403	shop	7
404	shot	5
405	shred	1
406	shreds	1
407	shrill	2
408	shrills	2
409	shrub	1
410	shrugs	9
411	sibling	1
412	sifts	1
413	silk	19
414	sink	1
415	sinking	1
416	sinks	4
417	sips	1
418	sit	5
419	sits	4
420	sitting	1
421	six	3
422	skid	1
423	skunk	1
424	slab	1
425	slaps	1

#	Word	Count
426	slip	3
427	slipping	1
428	slips	3
429	slog	1
430	smash	1
431	smith	6
432	smiths	18
433	snacks	1
434	snap	2
435	snaps	1
436	sniffs	2
437	snug	2
438	so	22
439	sobs	2
440	speck	1
441	specks	1
442	spell	4
443	spelling	37
444	spells	11
445	spill	1
446	spills	1
447	spins	1
448	split	2
449	splits	1
450	spot	20

#	Word	Count
451	spots	8
452	springs	1
453	sprints	3
454	squints	7
455	stack	2
456	stamps	1
457	stand	5
458	stands	5
459	stash	1
460	stay	1
461	stays	1
462	stem	4
463	step	7
464	steps	7
465	stick	2
466	sticking	1
467	sticks	3
468	still	32
469	stings	1
470	stock	1
471	stomps	4
472	stop	21
473	stops	7
474	strength	2
475	string	1

#	Word	Count
476	strips	1
477	stuck	9
478	stuff	1
479	stunning	1
480	stuns	1
481	such	1
482	sucks	2
483	summit	1
484	sun	24
485	sunkid	1
486	sunset	5
487	swift	1
488	swing	1
489	swings	2
490	tan	1
491	taps	9
492	tell	21
493	telling	1
494	tells	31
495	ten	2
496	text	1
497	texts	1
498	thank	1
499	thanks	2
500	that	55

#	Word	Count
501	the	620
502	their	5
503	them	29
504	then	45
505	there	22
506	they	88
507	thick	4
508	thicket	3
509	thin	1
510	thing	4
511	things	6
512	think	27
513	thinks	5
514	this	70
515	thrill	3
516	thud	3
517	tilts	1
518	tint	2
519	tip	1
520	to	215
521	top	6
522	track	1
523	trap	8
524	trek	3
525	trekking	1

#	Word	Count
526	trick	2
527	tricks	1
528	trip	4
529	trust	4
530	tucks	2
531	tugs	1
532	Twigs	57
533	twist	1
534	twists	2
535	unless	1
536	unlock	1
537	until	10
538	up	43
539	upset	3
540	us	35
541	vanish	2
542	visit	6
543	visiting	1
544	want	3
545	was	35
546	way	6
547	we	142
548	web	1
549	well	32
550	went	3

#	Word	Count
551	were	12
552	west	2
553	wet	3
554	what	50
555	when	35
556	where	25
557	who	1
558	why	4
559	will	83
560	win	4
561	wind	7
562	wing	3
563	wings	7
564	winks	2
565	wish	17
566	wishing	1
567	with	65
568	wits	1
569	yanks	3
570	yell	2
571	yelling	1
572	yells	24
573	yelps	3
574	yes	13
575	yet	4

#	Word	Count
576	you	110
577	your	8
578	yum	1
579	zips	1
Total Words		**8202**

Do you want to write your own story now?

Written by:

Do you want to draw your own story now?

Illustrated by:

WANT TO READ
MORE
CHAPTER BOOKS

7096 Words
Spelling Pen
in Elf Land
by C.Knebel

The Gold of
Black Rock Hill
by C. Knebel

4497 Words
SAM IS STUCK
BONUS
Includes
Comprehension
Workbook
by Çigdem Knebel

FOX HUNT
by Cigdem Knebel

Six Days at Camp
8369 Words
With Jack
and Max
by Cigdem Knebel

Six Days at Camp
8476 Words
With Lin and Jill
by Cigdem Knebel

STUDY GUIDES
AND
HANDBOOKS

www.simplewordsbooks.com

SIMPLE WORDS
✓Fluency
✓Comprehension
✓Self-Confidence

Decodable Chapter Books
We Choose Our Words Wisely

Spelling Pen in Elf Land
Comprehension Workbook

by C.Knebel

SIMPLE WORDS
✓Fluency
✓Comprehension
✓Self-Confidence

Decodable Chapter Books
We Choose Our Words Wisely

Spelling Pen
Red Obelisk
Comprehension Workbook

by C.Knebel

SIMPLE WORDS
✓Fluency
✓Comprehension
✓Self-Confidence

Decodable Chapter Books
We Choose Our Words Wisely

SAM IS STUCK
Phonics Workbook

by Cigdem Knebel

SIMPLE WORDS
✓Fluency
✓Comprehension
✓Self-Confidence

Decodable Chapter Books
We Choose Our Words Wisely

SAM IS STUCK
Comprehension Workbook

by Cigdem Knebel

SIMPLE WORDS
✓Fluency
✓Comprehension
✓Self-Confidence

Decodable Chapter Books
We Choose Our Words Wisely

BACK TO THE PAST
Comprehension Workbook

by Cigdem Knebel

SIMPLE WORDS
✓Fluency
✓Comprehension
✓Self-Confidence

Decodable Chapter Books
We Choose Our Words Wisely

FOX HUNT
Comprehension Workbook

by Cigdem Knebel

VISIT OUR WEBSITE FOR FREE RESOURCES

simplewordsbooks.com

AND CHECK OUT OUR FREE ONLINE SUMMITS

Printed in Great Britain
by Amazon